Compilation copyright © 1990 by Dick Bruna Books, Inc.
Illustrations Dick Bruna, copyright © Mercis bv, 1963, 1964, 1968, 1969, 1972, 1974, 1979, 1980, 1982

Created and manufactured by Dick Bruna Books, Inc., by arrangement with Ottenheimer Publishers, Inc. Illustrations by Dick Bruna.
No part of this book may be reproduced in any form without written permission from the publisher.

First published in Great Britain in 1990 by William Collins Sons & Co Ltd, 8 Grafton Street, London W1X 3LA

A CIP catalogue record for this book is available from the British Library

0 00 184580 2

Printed in Italy

I know my opposites

Dick Bruna

COLLINS

open

closed

big

small

many

few

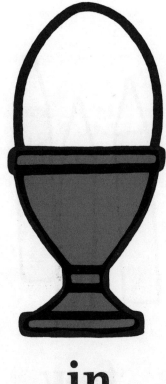

in

out

happy

sad

up

down

front

back

tall

short

alike

different

on

off

come

go

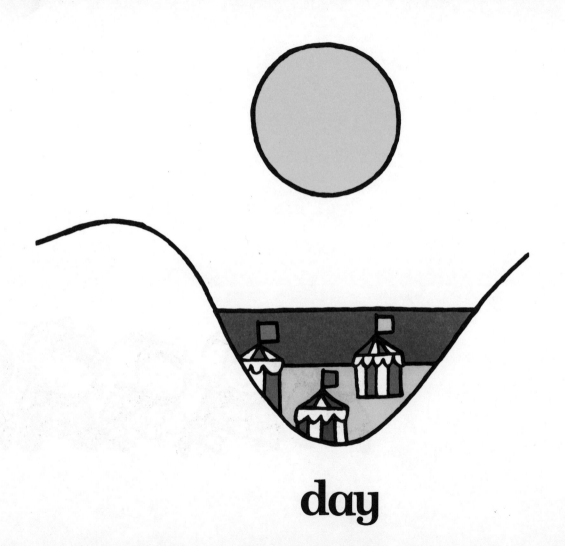

day

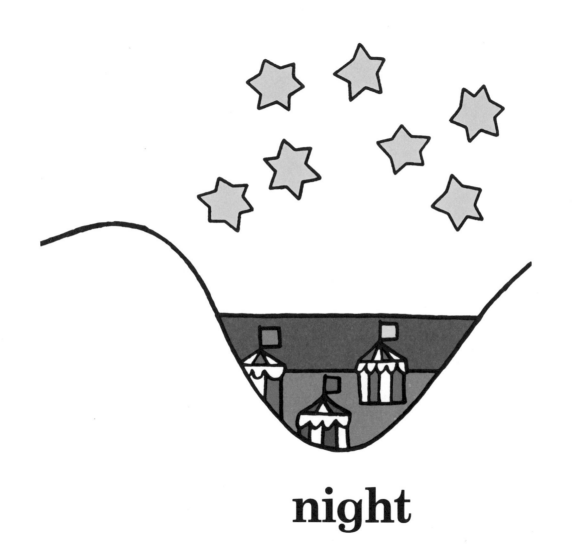

night